WHIMSICAL POETRY

FICTION AND REALITY

SYEDA JAVERIA FATIMA

First and foremost, The Almighty God has been kind. In the process of putting this book together, I recognized how incredible this souvenir of writing is for me.

I especially want to thank the individuals that cared for making this happen.

My parents Dr.Syed Yousufuddin and Munawar Sultana for providing wisdom, zeal, assistance, and opportunities that have made me who I am. Because of their endeavors and encouragement, I have a legacy to pass on to my family where one didn't prevail before.

My sisters Syeda Amina Sultana and Syeda Noor Fatima, for not just reckoning, but understanding that I could do this!

My family for their unparalleled support and effective criticism.

My friends are my extended family and without their enthusiasm, it wouldn't have been possible!

This one's for you all.

Lastly, I want to thank EVERYONE who said anything optimistic to me or enlightened me about something. I heard it all, and it symbolized something.

You know what, and you probably know why!

Contents

Preface

Oh, dear readers! I'd like to convey through my poetry, the emotions that I've held in my arms. The belief whose seal has to be broken yet. A collection of bittersweet poetry that I've either imagined or witnessed with my own eyes.

What emotions does our mind construct? How do societal issues shun a set of people? Is it that difficult to feel empathy? Is happiness a myth or have we often believed so? Is it family that one seeks? How does friendship last over time? What do a poet's eyes see and what do their mind grab?

All these questions shall be countered as you shall proceed in this book.

Casually walk in, and take a look around!

1.

Let yourself start again, over and over, as often as needed!

MY BELIEF

A leap of faith as I take,

Through small undertakings, my thirst I slake.

Never felt life could pull an unexpected brake,

Panic-stricken, my body began to shake.

As my heart thumped, I flashed a smile,

no one hinted it was fake.

I dreamt whilst being wide awake,

Soon to admit, this is life with no retake.

From out of nowhere, I was blessed,

To be optimistic and not be stressed.

An appealing thought crossed my mind,

What would I do, if The Almighty God hadn't been so kind?

He steered me through when I acted blind,

So I decide to let go without pressing rewind!

-faith over negativity

Life isn't always sunshine and smiles,

sometimes it heals after rain and pain

and suffering and moving on.

Hear me out...

Feel gratitude in your soul

for all that's around.

Tap into the magic

that's waiting to be found.

THAT'S MY MOTHER

I know a woman so audacious and brave,

for every task she did, her best she gave.

An epitome of fondness, paths of gold she paved!

A perfect homemaker, an all-rounder,

who performs her duties with glee.

Whose daughters are her priority,

Yet for not having a son,

she's looked upon with sympathy.

From her side, the sympathy was paid no heed,

Parity is something in which she believed.

Such negativity shall be freed!

And she reckons;

Certainly, a day will come,

A world to witness full of optimism.

Where positivity shall dominate negativity,

Declaring the victory of liberty over inequality!

-written by the daughter of a valiant mother that raised her

*

She's such a woman, with a smile, the world she conquered.

2. THE SERIES

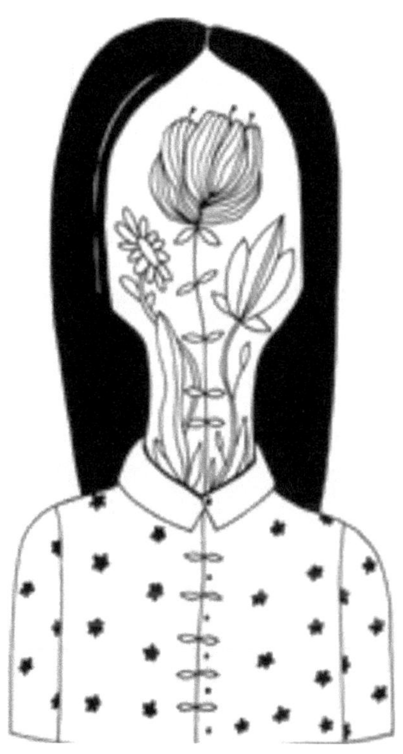

- *INCESSANT LOVE: The girl is describing the person she loves*
- *THE SILENT WARRIOR: Here, she receives a eulogy from her loved one.*

INCESSANT LOVE (Part-1)

The modest green chlorophyll skin,
exhibited their summer veins.
Just like nature,
too gorgeous enough,
at once made my heart snug.
The exotic eyes, jovial smile,
rejuvenates me and so much more.
That's the way, them I adore!

Makes me laugh and
makes me cry.
When they're around,
it's never a bleak moment.
A million stories those eyes tell,
The night we met,
Prudent in my heart
those tales dwell.
Just like an ancient attic,
stabilized in my heart's basement!

ONE SUCH PROMISE

(THE SEQUEL)

Calm you, exuberant me,
never-ending laughter,
beauteous memories,
With you by my side,
together forever.
Bonding of ours,
ever to cherish.
This is the promise I want to keep.

But now,
Life appears hoax,
With my days numbered and
moments left, few to honour.
To my shock, it's a horror.
You want me to live,
to be by your side,
as I had testified earlier.
It's enervating, as I say,
this is the promise I can't keep.

Although, I want you to promise me,

that you'll write me a eulogy,

how unjust it was for me and you,

with our love story taken to a halt.

stating the Fault in Our Stars,

and unobtrusive scars which only you saw.

Now kiss me goodbye and

let me sleep in peace.

THE SILENT WARRIOR

(THE FINALE)

For me she was special,
The bond we shared
made it evidential.
She had silky long hair,
her skin so flawless and fair.
Those sparkling, alluring eyes,
spoke volume all the time.
Maybe intoxicated with love
which filled my life
with a positive reprise.
Every time she held my hand,
my problems seemed
to surcease.
As I saw her smile appear,
I noticed negativity disappear.
We had our language, words to speak,
new phrases, and words every week.

Writing this now,
I'm on the verge of tears.

My heart cries, so do my eyes!

So many things left unsaid,

No wonder why my insides feel dead!

Every grueling step she took in her stride,

Even at her lowest, I'm proud she tried.

Didn't God see how much it would hurt?

To and fro, as I walk through the corridor,

I try to act as if I don't care anymore.

She was my beloved gone too soon.

But I still wear the smile

she gave me that monsoon!

She laughs with essence and cries in metaphors.

Challenges the atrocities of her life,

narrates it through her fervent poetry!

3. MY ALMA MATER

The journey so far from the world unseen to becoming a teen wasn't easy.
Top-notch excuses we made,
Within ourselves, we discovered a new shade.
Lessons were learned from the mistakes we made.
Sharing and caring were the emotions we played.

In the same boat together we sailed.
Some friends were shuffled,

but they struggled and proved their metal.
Sharing tiffins was a trend,
how I wish those memories I could lend.
Teachers were ever tolerant,
never giving up was their spirit,
making us work harder was their tactic.

This year was a combo of sweet and spice,
thriller, and comedy.
Not submitting work on time was the biggest tragedy!
These memories take me down the lane,
many valuable experiences I've gained.
The pleasing spectacle at one excites,
such recollection of our delights.
That viewing it, we seem almost to obtain,
Our sweet, crazy, innocent years again!

.

.

.

.

.

.

.

-a piece of my heart <3

DESCRIBE YOUR SCHOOL LIFE IN ONE/FEW WORDS!

(Here are a few responses I collected...)

#1 My school life wasn't completely a top-notch yet gave me a lot of memories to cherish.

#2 It was a roller coaster ride tbh and that school vibe was sooo different and magical it's been 5 years and i can still feel those unforgettable vibes

#3 Brooo was littttt , it was kiraaakkkk the bestest time of my life I had huge group of friends set study thingyy , oh btw I am from ICSE so my English is top notch it's From my school ... It Wass litttt !!

#4 decent, i dont think about it much or infact i dont think or reminisce about it at all

#5 My school days were vibrant and full of colour.I can confidently say that those were some of the best days of my life.I enjoyed going to school and meeting friends.We used to have lots of events at school which taught me lots of lessons and were also fun

#6 Emotions

#7 School life- enjoyable

#8 Lots of fun. Innocence. Creative

4. STARGAZING

Late at night, the stars I gaze.
The reason for my craze,
efficiently worth my praise.
Up in the sky supreme,
How irresistibly they gleam!
Quiet contentment and a nirvana full of stars.
Am I awake or living a dream?
Turns sadness into happiness,
guess that's the scheme!
Pessimistic thoughts to me no longer bother,
My sorrows seem to surcease in one way or another.
Just then, swayed cool breeze,
left me longing with such ease.
It's the peace that I harbor,
my heart feels a lot warmer.
I adore the gleaming sky with my eyes,
The night of summer is a total reprise!

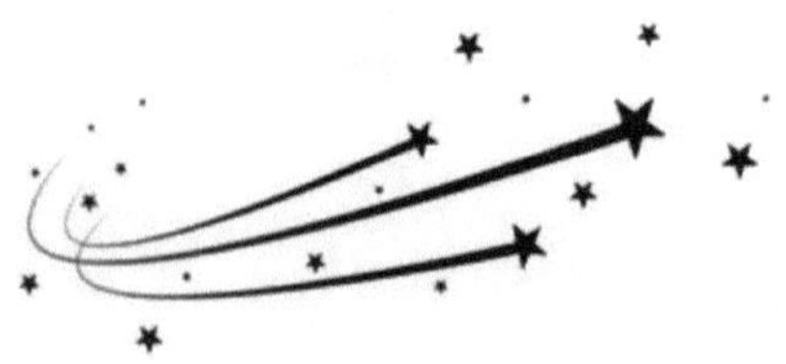

"Look at the stars and look at you, both a treat to my eyes!"

.

Mental peace over anything. PERIOD.

5. DEPLORABLE REALITY

We live in a country where;

Democracy cries,
Unity ultimately divides.
Nirbhaya was India's daughter,
yet her justice was delayed.
Men aren't safe either,
yet we delude
things never happen
and ignore them effortlessly.
The wealthy with all privileges,
compete to be the best.
With people impoverished and
their hardships unaddressed.

We live in a society where;
It's communal riots over composure,
where none can justify their
awful behavior.
Sexism and racism are
misconstrued as sarcasm,
Pseudo-feminism is

the new rendition of feminism.
Such are the issues received
with no enthusiasm.
The depressed are
validated weak
and you're preposterous
if ethically you speak.
<>
Instead...
It should be a country where;
Unity remains.
Democracy prevails,
Justice is served.
miseries disappear,
and harmony reappears.
.
Peace over riots,
Judging someone disregarded.
Being sexist and racist doesn't make you affable.
Feminism is the parallelism of all genders.
Depression is considered profound
and when such issues are raised,
People who address it aren't absurd!!!!

6. FRIENDSHIP

Look what I have to say as such.
From detesting you to evolving best friends,
our friendship came on a long path.
Over a span of time,
I got to know the actual you.
With a heart that was true,
ultimately the bond grew.
And that's when I knew,
how fortunate I am to have you.

With your smile so innocent,
those intentions could be felt.
You valued little things I did,
But never boast of what you attained.
And when I texted jibber-jabber,
I bet you thought I'd never end.
Our conversations are a blend of giggles and laughter,
I still wonder how you texted me whenever I began to falter.
Was it telepathy?
I believe it was pure courtesy.

For putting on my face a smile,
you nearly went the extra mile.

Happy times, night and day,
Such remembrances will never fade away.
From happiness to strife,
Wouldn't swap it for anything else in life.
Like a tree, you stood sturdy,
provided feelings of solace and safety.
When times were harsh and I was down,
You were one of those who stuck around.
And for that, I dedicate this poem to you
and tell you from my heart,
I LOVE YOU!!!

7. INSECURITIES

What am I insecure about?
Is it my boisterous voice?
Or tears that others rejoice?
Is it my forgetful behavior?
Or the things that I yearn to remember?
Is it my crooked smile that I forbid?
Or how effortlessly my sadness I hid?
What am I insecure about?
But today,
I woke up with thoughts vetoing my insecurities,
Declaring the victory of my sureties.
My thoughts now clearer,
fill me up with a calm demeanor.
I laugh wholeheartedly with essence,
And no longer question my existence!

If only you realize that it's all your "flaws" that set you apart and make your character distinctive. Remember that you are loved regardless of them. Don't let anyone tell you otherwise!

What is one flaw that you have embraced wholeheartedly?*(Here are a few responses I collected...)*

#1 | I constantly have the thought of changing myself and become better. I wish to erase Every flaw that I have but I know nobody is perfect and these flaws complete me, make me who I am. So now that you've asked me this question, I will try and start embracing my flaws.

#2 | Soo my height is the most avg height one can find in world, and the thing i don't like is being average soo yeah my height sometimes made me uncomfortable

#3 | not listening to what good others have for me or whatever they advice me to only ending up following what i think is right or in my interest. cant say it's something ive embraced wholeheartedly, but its something that i know wont change

#4 | I have this "to be liked" wala syndrome like everyone around me should like me , ik it's very not realistic but it's something I don't wanna loose it's kinda me !

#5 | Self imperfections

#6 | Being tardy i feel so good being late everywhere

8. BREAK THE BIAS

"It's a daughter, not again!"
Many people sigh with pain.
Love and fondness, she wants to gain,
but her practices are all in vain.
For a boy, the parents pray,
the daughter's life is painted black and grey.
Memories without love, years forlorn.
Only pleads to God, for her destiny re-written.
What is her fault I ask today?
Don't you see her die a little, every day?
God never differentiated who deserves love and who doesn't,
then why do we humans live with a mentality that ferments?
She is a blessing sent from above,
help her showcase her hidden potential.
Love her because she is entitled to it,
Give her the freedom of speech,
and the rights she never heard of.
Let's do the bare minimum,
as everyone is empowered to do it.

“"I wish that from today,
you hustle to fight your demons
and set yourself free!"”

9. YOU AND ME

This is a story of us:

guilty for the manifestations of fortune,
guilty for the awful as well.

.

guilty for spending time,
guilty for saving time.

.

guilty for being unable to sleep.
guilty for napping till late.

.

guilty for being stressed,
guilty for causing stress.

.

guilty for dining full,
guilty for filling stomach half.

.

guilty for not focussing on studies,
guilty for not exploring enough talent.

.

guilty for the affordable,
guilty for the luxuries.

.

guilty for thoughts not whining,
guilty for overthinking as well.

.

Are we content or pretending to be?
guess we'll never know!

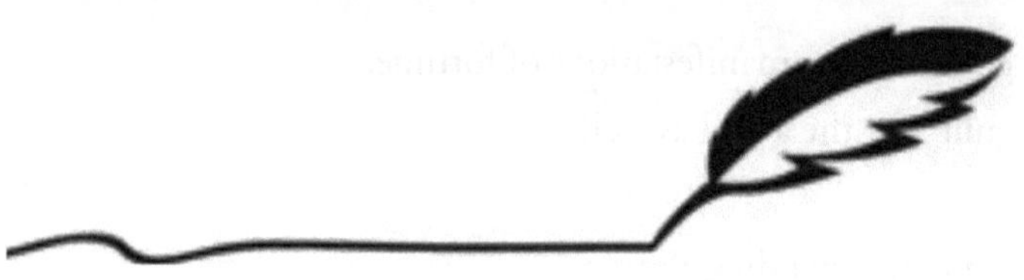

10. MY BESTFRIENDS

My two best friends since childhood,
forever close to my heart.
Often inseparable,
genuinely adorable.
Their sermons applaudable
made my life remarkable.
Their presence ever approachable
made any crisis endurable.
Their traits are admirable,
temperament is just phenomenal.
Their memories invaluable,
certainly unforgettable.

.

Always reminded me,
that I had walls to tear,
fears to conquer, that's the dare.
To spread love and laughter,
to be generous and sincere.
Guided me with permutations rare,
to be content and never compare.
Whenever I needed them, they were there,
even edified me to care.
Ever pragmatic, fair, and square.

.

I say this with a void in my heart,
God chose to impart, a brutal plan to compart.
On the 17th Day Of Ramadan, Nana breathed his last.
"I can't keep you two apart, now you too shall depart."
And just 11 days after, on the 28th of Ramadan,
unaware of her beloved passing away, Nani left us too.
Only if life had a contract to renew!
I seldom believed in soulmates,
but now I thoroughly do.
Learned a lot from them as I grew,
Honestly, people like them are few!

.

The remembrances in my heart intact,
on me, they had a huge impact.
Made sure to understand me,
loved me profoundly and that's a fact.
To be young at heart, an example they set.
My grandparents, my human diaries I recollect.
Taught me to be grounded,
saved me from getting scolded.
An episode from my daily life,
full-on drama one could say.
Not just today,
I remember them every day.
My two best friends since childhood,
forever close to my heart.

"I see your pictures/ videos
and smile endlessly.
Only to surrender that
you don't surround me anymore!"

01

"Desire what you want
and it shall come true
You possess the ability
and it's always in YOU."

02

My friend, you are stronger than you give yourself credit for! The world needs just you being you with all the **potential** waiting to be explored! <3

9 798886 298468

Printed by Libri Plureos GmbH in Hamburg, Germany